EXPLORATIONS

# REACHING THE NORTH POLE

BY DALTON RAINS

WWW.APEXEDITIONS.COM



Apex is distributed by North Star Editions:
sales@northstareditions.com | 888-417-0195

Produced for Apex by Red Line Editorial.

Photographs ©: Bettmann/Getty Images, cover, 25, 26–27; Shutterstock Images, 1, 4–5, 7, 16–17, 22–23; Library of Congress, 6, 10–11, 15, 29; ullstein bild Dtl./Getty Images, 8–9; Hulton Archive/Getty Images, 12–13; Robert Peary/Hulton Archive/Getty Images, 14; Hulton Archive/Archive Photos/Getty Images, 19; General Photographic Agency/Hulton Archive/Getty Images, 20–21; iStockphoto, 24

**Library of Congress Control Number: 2024912899**

**ISBN**
979-8-89250-332-7 (hardcover)
979-8-89250-370-9 (paperback)
979-8-89250-443-0 (ebook pdf)
979-8-89250-408-9 (hosted ebook)

Printed in the United States of America
Mankato, MN
012025

## NOTE TO PARENTS AND EDUCATORS

**Apex books are designed to build literacy skills in striving readers. Exciting, high-interest content attracts and holds readers' attention. The text is carefully leveled to allow students to achieve success quickly. Additional features, such as bolded glossary words for difficult terms, help build comprehension.**

# TABLE OF CONTENTS

# CHAPTER 1

# RACE TO THE POLE

People began trying to reach the North Pole in the 1800s. Many failed. But in the early 1900s, two groups claimed to make it.

The North Pole is the spot at the very top of planet Earth.

Frederick Cook led the first group. He sailed to Greenland in 1907. There, nine **Inuit** joined him. They set off for the Pole in February 1908. They rode dogsleds over the ice.

**Frederick Cook worked as a doctor before becoming an explorer.**

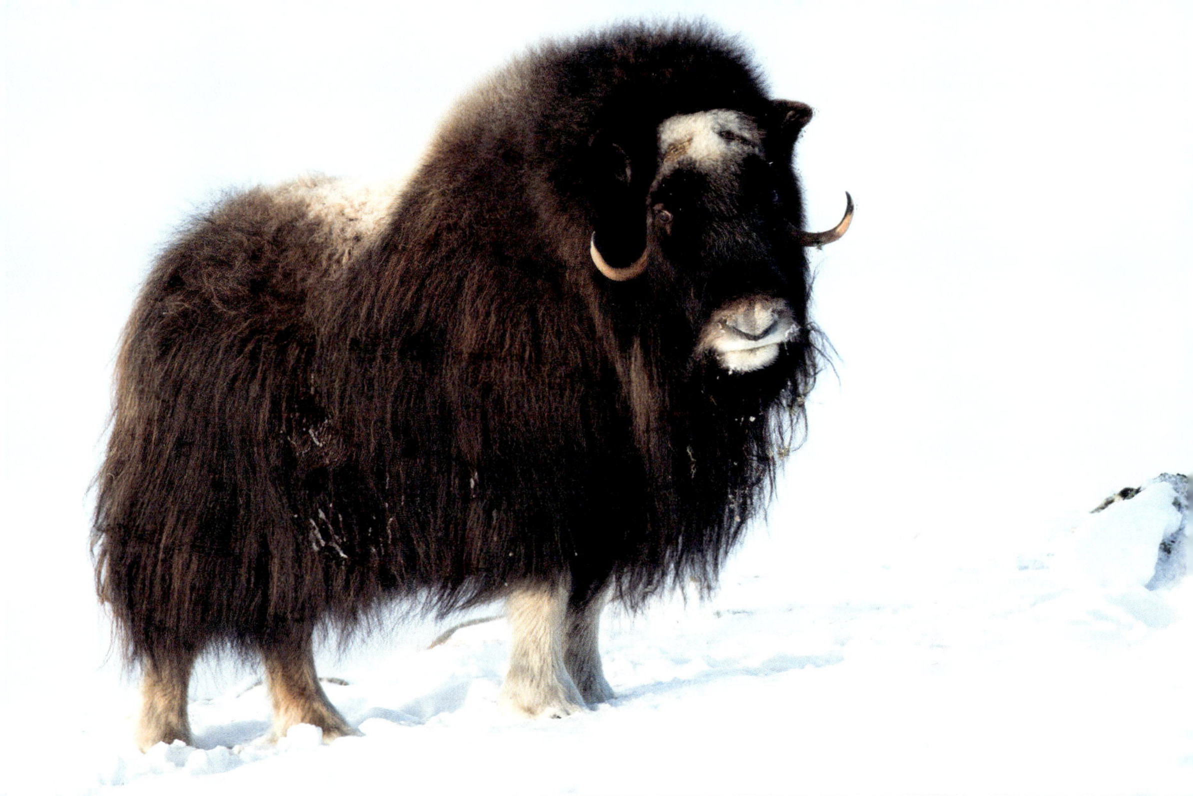

Cook's group ate musk oxen during their journey. These large animals live in cold, northern areas.

FAST FACT

Cook's group used 11 sleds. They were pulled by 103 dogs.

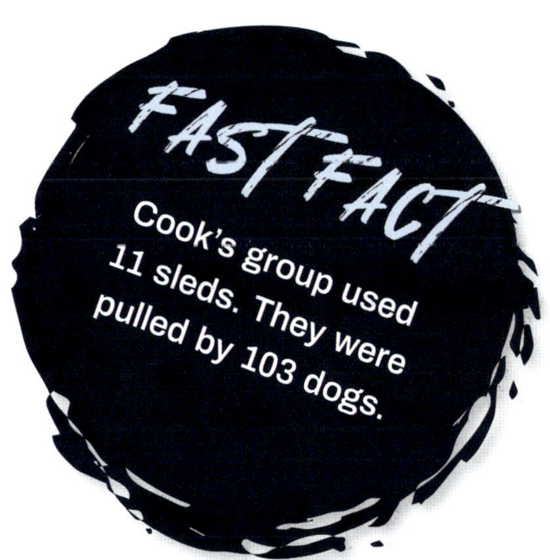

Cook's small group traveled 360 miles (580 km) in 24 days. He said they stayed at the Pole for two days.

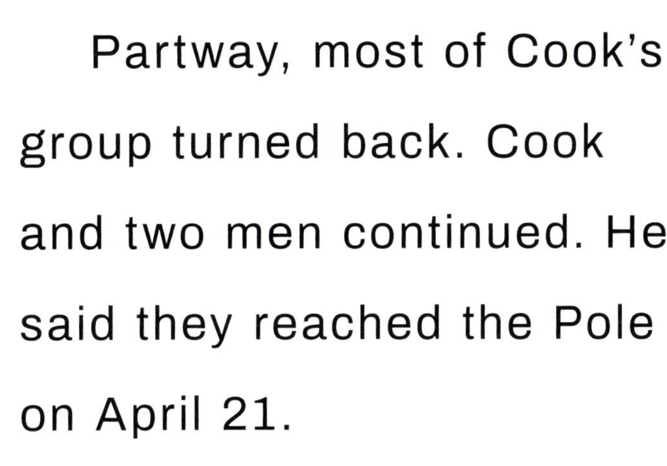

Partway, most of Cook's group turned back. Cook and two men continued. He said they reached the Pole on April 21.

## TRICKY TARGET

Earth's South Pole is on land. But the North Pole is on sea ice. This ice moves around. To find the North Pole, people must measure **latitude**. The Pole is at 90 degrees north.

# CHAPTER 2

# ANOTHER ATTEMPT

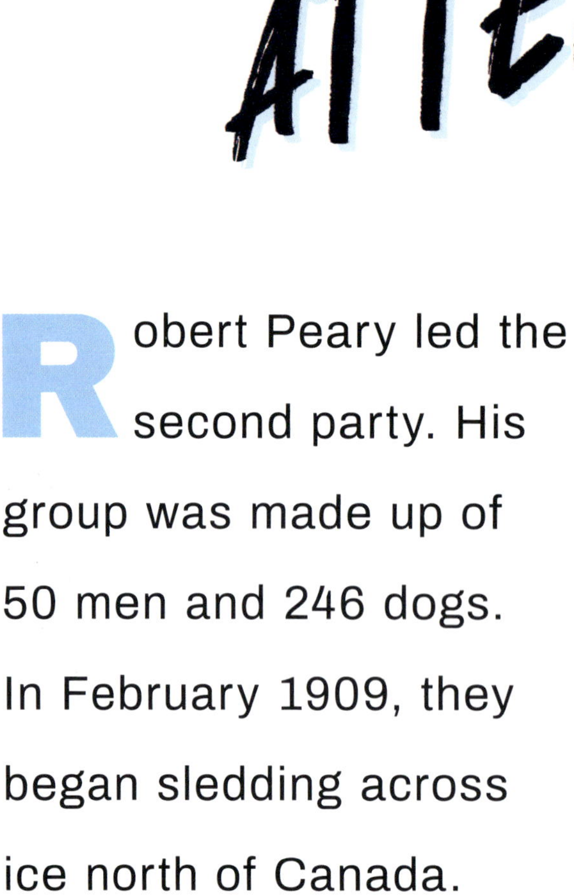

Robert Peary led the second party. His group was made up of 50 men and 246 dogs. In February 1909, they began sledding across ice north of Canada.

Between 1886 and 1909, Robert Peary made eight trips to areas near the North Pole.

They soon faced problems. Patches of open water blocked their path. They had to wait for the ice to refreeze. Sometimes this took days.

FAST FACT

Peary's party traveled an average of 13 miles (21 km) per day.

Some of Peary's sleds went ahead. They left supplies for the rest of the team.

For the journey's last leg, Peary brought just five men. He checked a **sextant**. But he didn't tell the others what it said. He claimed they reached the North Pole on April 6, 1909.

Peary's group took a picture when they thought they reached the North Pole.

**Matthew Henson traveled at the front of the group. He helped the other sleds find the way.**

## SMALL GROUP

Peary's small group included four Inuit guides and Matthew Henson. Henson was a Black American explorer. He had helped Peary lead several other **expeditions**.

# CHAPTER 3

# DEBATED CLAIMS

Meanwhile, drifting ice and cold weather delayed Cook's return. He reached Greenland in April 1909. He said his team succeeded.

People thought sea ice near the North Pole would move east. But it carried Cook's group west.

Peary said Cook was lying. He said only his team reached the Pole. Many **investigations** followed. For years, most people agreed with Peary. Today, most experts think that neither group made it.

## PROOF PROBLEMS

Cook kept notes during his journey. But some got lost. In 1988, scientists studied more of Peary's notes. They learned he probably didn't go all the way to the Pole.

**Newspapers reported on the conflict between Cook and Peary. Some took sides.**

"...e News That's ...to Print."

# The New York Times.

THE WEATHER. Warmer, increasing cloudiness to-day; showers to-morrow.

NO. 18,856. NEW YORK, THURSDAY, SEPTEMBER 9, 1909.—TWENTY PAGES. ONE CENT

## NOT NEAR POLE, SAYS PEARY; PROOFS STILL HELD BACK BY COOK

...d by Cook Told ...r Went Far ...and.

..."OOK NAILED"

...Not to Worry ...tor's Claim ...Pole.

...R AN INQUIRY

...bmit His Ob-... Competent ...ts.

...TORY GROWS

...proofs that he had visited the north pole on April 21, 1908. Those proofs were convincing and would in due time be given to the world.

**Doesn't Fear Public Clamor.**

When it was suggested to him that his chances of proving his case might be ruined unless he made a satisfactory statement immediately, he smiled—his usual quiet smile, and asked how could a man be ruined by popular clamor calling him an imposter when he had proofs in his case which could and would be published, as he had ofttimes repeated, when they were in proper form to be given out.

Dr. Cook told Capt. Sverdrup and another friend the day after he landed here that he hoped there would be no unpleasantness over supplies with the Peary party; that he had found some of Peary's men in possession of one of his depots and had turned them out unceremoniously.

It is settled that Cook will send a ship back to bring to America the two Eskimos who accompanied him on the last stage of his journey to the pole, as well as some of the party who were sent back when the start of the last stage began. Capt. Sverdrup may command the expedition. It is Dr. Cook's desire that he shall do so, and they conferred for some hours to-day regarding the details of the expedition.

Dr. Cook's purpose in bringing his Eskimo comrades to America is to have them relate their stories of the trip to the pole. He proposes to have them examined by any men familiar with the arctic and the Eskimo, including the members of Commander Peary's party, if they wish. Dr. Cook's apparent confidence is the greatest factor working in his support in Copenhagen. Those who have had the opportunity to talk with him are only of one mind, that he is an absolutely sincere, simple man, or deserves a pedestal in history as one of the greatest of actors.

### PROOFS TO-DAY, SAYS COOK.

**But Grave Doubt Is Felt That He Can Supply Them.**

By PHILIP GIBBS.

Special Cable to THE NEW YORK TIMES. Dispatch to The London Daily Chronicle.

COPENHAGEN, Sept. 8.—The most profound sensation was produced and great excitement prevailed to-day in Copenhagen after Dr. Cook's [illegible] last night. People who would have staked their lives upon his honesty were now full of the most terrible doubts. The lecture was a fiasco of the first magnitude and seemed so obviously a story of the imagination, wildly improbable and unsupported by a shred of scientific facts, that those many explorers who were present in this city of explorers and who stood by Cook now felt shattered in their belief. Some of them went to Cook early this morning and told him that unless he produced the strongest evidence of his claim within twenty-four hours they would denounce him as an impostor. To this he said:

"I will produce my proofs within twenty-four hours."

Immediately after that declaration Peary's telegrams were published in Copenhagen. The effect was immediately seen in the Danish newspapers. They had upheld Dr. Cook, and had denounced me personally for my daily criticism of Cook's story. Now they come out with articles headed "Is Cook an Impostor?" and Danish journalists came to interview the English journalist who had been alone in his disbelief. That was the only amusing thing in a day which had been [illegible] exciting and too strenuous. I had many things to do. I had first of all to see Cook himself and ask him what he had to say about Peary's words. He said:

"I shall say very little about what Peary says. It does not matter to me. Wait a little while and you will see."

I must now say that this man Frederick Cook is the most remarkable, most amazing man I have ever met. He calls me his enemy, but I have no personal animosity against him, and I will say honestly that I am filled with a sense of profound admiration for him. If he is an impostor he is also a very brave man—a man with such iron nerve, such miraculous self-control, and such magnificent courage in playing a game, that he will count for ever among the greatest impostors of the world. That and not the discovery of the north [illegible] shall be his claim to immortality.

Here was this man flouted by all who had acclaimed him a hero, with his story strongly discounted by Peary, [illegible] by circumstantial evidence, and threatened within twenty-four hours by the [illegible] of final exposure, and yet he faced the world, defied criticism, and smiled and smiled again.

everything, and I shall prove the truth of my story to the world."

To these words I say Cook cannot prove his story to-morrow or the day after. Cook has no proof in Copenhagen to give the university, and if the committee which is to make the examination says, "We are satisfied," then I say beforehand they will be satisfied without proof, without any trustworthy evidence whatever, as Prof. Stromgren was satisfied without proof or evidence, because I had evidence to-day still further proving that Cook cannot produce proof to-morrow. I had that evidence from one of the most distinguished men of science in Europe, whose word cannot be doubted, and who still believes, or tries to believe, in Cook, and I had that evidence from Frederick Cook himself. I will give briefly the gist of two remarkable interviews, first with Dr. de Querlain, Chief of the Swiss-German expedition and joint Director of the Swiss Central Meteorological Institute. This interview was before three witnesses and the special correspondent of a London journal, Comte de Lesdain, and myself. The following questions were asked and answered:

"Do you know Cook well?"

"I was four weeks with him. Upon his return, coming back with him in the Hans Egede, we had long conversations."

"Did he show you any of his observations?"

"No; but he said he would show them to me. I pointed out to him the importance of putting forward proofs to satisfy public opinion, and it was for that reason I suggested he should show me his observations, as, of course, I have had long training experience in these matters."

"And did he?"

"No. I regret to say that when I asked him again he said he would prefer not to do so."

**No Observations on Hans Egede.**

"Are you sure he had any observations on board?"

"I could not be sure. He had a box on board in which he said he had papers. Most of his books went by boat—Whitney's boat—from Greenland to America."

"Would it be possible for him to make imaginary observations?"

[illegible] but it would be very difficult."

"Did he have proper instruments with him?"

"He had a sextant and chronometers."

"Was this sextant an ordinary one?"

"He told me it was a better sextant than the ordinary one used in the navy."

"Has he brought his instruments to Copenhagen?"

"No, he sent them to America."

"But is it not necessary to test these instruments before the value of the observations can be proved?"

"Strictly speaking, that is so."

After this interview, in which every answer was drawn painfully and reluctantly from a man desiring to shield his friend but compelled by conscience to tell the truth, Dr. de Quervain signed a document in which he made this remarkable statement. The following are his exact words:

"I recognise that Cook, with whom I passed several weeks on board the Hans Egede, has given me the impression of a man who understands quite well how to take observations. Moreover, Knud Rasmussen, who passed some time with Cook after the return of the latter from the pole, has received favorable evidence of Cook's story from Eskimos who knew two men who accompanied Cook and believes Cook has been to the pole.

**Didn't Tell of Meeting Rasmussen.**

The later part of his statement is startling. Cook never referred to his meeting with Rasmussen upon his homeward journey. Rasmussen's letter to his wife suggests a direct contradiction of Cook upon a material point, and from the lips of Mrs. Rasmussen and Mr. Freuchen, an explorer in whose hands I first saw this letter, I heard the words that Mr. Rasmussen does not believe in Cook's claim. They have repeated that to others.

This, however, is not part of my main argument. The essential point in the above interview is Cook's refusal to show Quervain his observations after his promise to do so. [illegible] ment that Cook's instruments and most of his books have been sent to America by way of Greenland. I now come to Cook himself. This morning I put the following questions to him in the presence of Comte de Lesdain.

"Have you any original observations in Copenhagen?"

"At first Cook refused to answer this question. He then said:

## COMMANDER PEARY'S PRELIMINARY ACCOUNT OF HIS SUCCESSFUL VOYAGE TO THE NORTH POLE

He Sends to The Times by Wireless a Summary, to be Followed by His Full Report—Record of His Swift Progress to the Utmost North.

## FROM CAPE COLUMBIA UP IN 37 DAYS, BACK IN 16 DAYS

Prof. Ross G. Marvin, of Cornell, Drowned on April 10, Forty-five Miles North of Cape Columbia, While Leading the Supporting Party.



BATTLE HARBOR, Labrador, Via Wireless Cape Ray, N. F., Sept. 8.—As it may be impossible to get my full story through in time for to-morrow's TIMES, partly as a prelude which may stimulate interest and partly to forestall possible leaks, I am sending you a brief summary of my voyage to the North Pole, which is to be printed exactly as written.

### SUMMARY OF NORTH POLAR EXPEDITION OF THE PEARY ARCTIC CLUB.

The steamer Roosevelt left New York on July 6, 1908; left Sydney on July 17; arrived at Cape York, Greenland, August 1; left Etah, Greenland, August 8; arrived Cape Sheridan, at Grantland, September 1; wintered at Cape Sheridan.

The sledge expedition left the Roosevelt February 15, 1909, and started for the North. Arrived at Cape Columbia March 1; passed British record March 2; delayed by open water March 2 and 3; held up by open water March 4 to 11; crossed the 84th parallel March 11; encountered open lead March 15; crossed 85th parallel March 18; crossed 86th parallel March 23d; encountered open lead March 23d; passed Norwegian record March 23d; passed Italian record March 24th; encountered open lead March 26th; crossed 87th parallel March 27th; passed American record March 28; encountered open lead March 28; held up by open water March 29; crossed 88th parallel April 2; crossed 89th parallel April 4; North Pole April 6.

All returning left North Pole April 7, reached Cape Columbia April 23, arriving on board Roosevelt April 27.

The Roosevelt left Cape Sheridan July 18, passed Cape Sabine August 8; left Cape York August 26; arrived at Indian Harbor with all members of expedition returning in good health except Prof. Ross G. Marvin, unfortunately drowned April 10, when forty-five miles north of Cape Columbia, returning from 86° North Latitude in command of the supporting party.

ROBERT E. PEARY.

### MAP SHOWING PEARY'S ROUTE TO THE POLE.

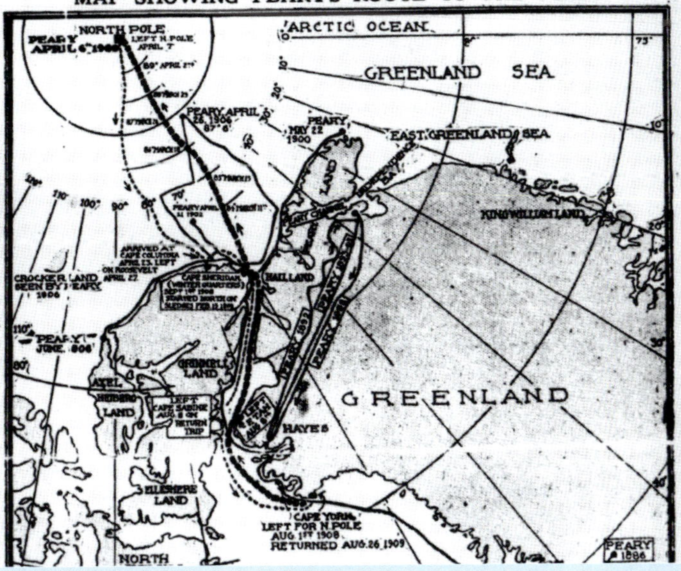

Other explorers tried flying to the Pole. Richard Byrd made several attempts. He said he flew over it on May 9, 1926. But his claim was disproved.

Richard Byrd's plane took off from Norway.

# CHAPTER 4

# CONFIRMED TRIPS

Roald Amundsen led the first team that reached the North Pole for sure. His group used an airship. It flew over the Pole on May 12, 1926.

Roald Amundsen's airship was called the *Norge*. It flew from islands near Norway over to Alaska.

**The Soviets used a type of plane called the Lisunov Li-2.**

In 1948, **Soviet** explorers landed three planes at the North Pole. They were the first people to touch the ground there.

FAST FACT

In 1958, a US submarine called the USS *Nautilus* became the first ship to reach the North Pole.

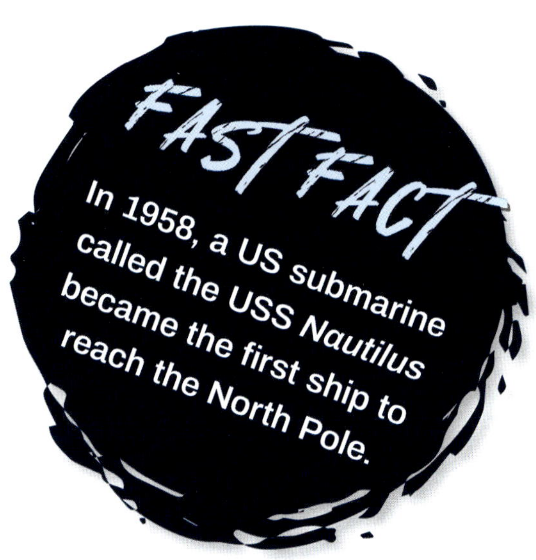

**The USS *Nautilus* made history by sailing under the North Pole's ice.**

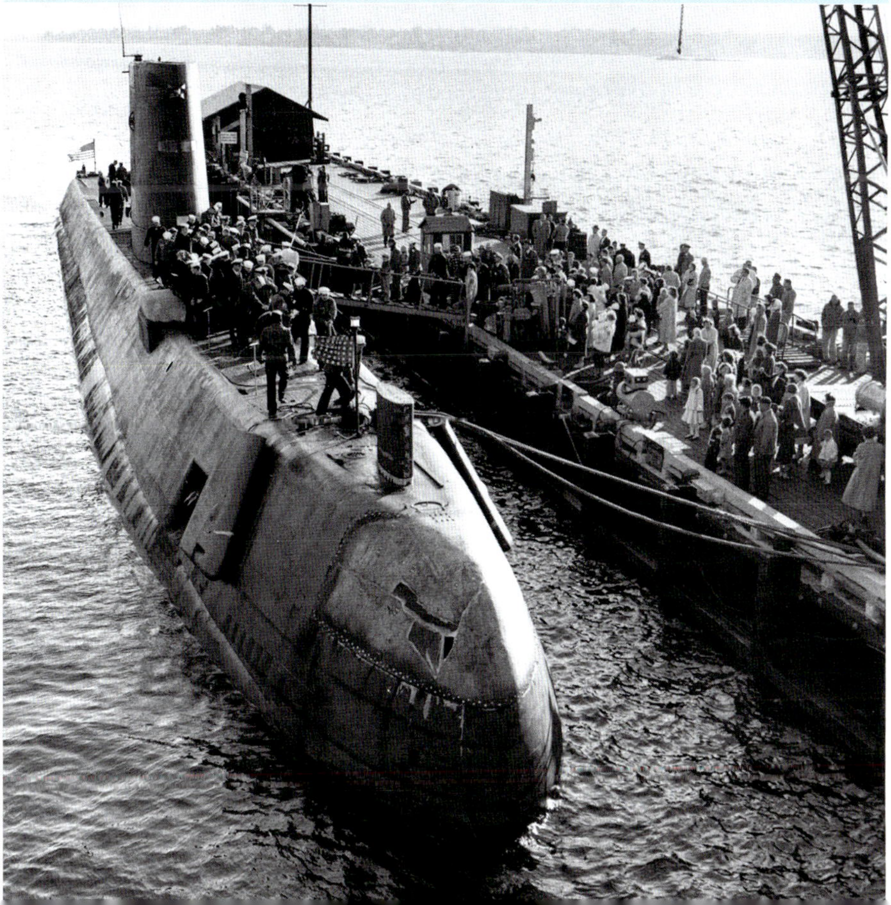

The first **confirmed** trip by land was in 1968. A group of Americans rode **snowmobiles**. They reached the North Pole on April 20.

## UNLIKELY GROUP

Ralph Plaisted led the 1968 group. He was from Minnesota. So were his team members. None were explorers before this trip. They did it because of a dare.

Before traveling to the North Pole, Ralph Plaisted was an insurance salesman.

# COMPREHENSION QUESTIONS

*Write your answers on a separate piece of paper.*

**1.** Write a few sentences describing the main ideas of Chapter 3.

**2.** Would you like to visit the North Pole? Why or why not?

**3.** When did Roald Amundsen fly over the North Pole?

- **A.** 1909
- **B.** 1926
- **C.** 1948

**4.** About how long did it take Cook's group to get back to Greenland from the North Pole?

- **A.** one month
- **B.** one year
- **C.** seven years

**5.** What does **attempts** mean in this book?

*Other explorers tried flying to the Pole. Richard Byrd made several **attempts**.*

A. times of waiting
B. ways to spend money
C. tries to reach a goal

**6.** What does **disproved** mean in this book?

*He said he flew over it on May 9, 1926. But his claim was **disproved**.*

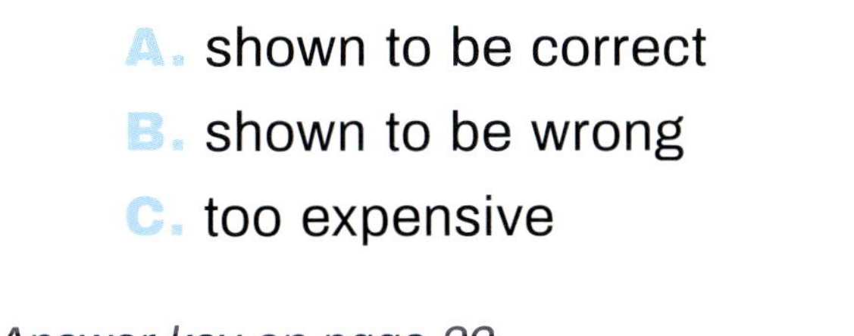

A. shown to be correct
B. shown to be wrong
C. too expensive

*Answer key on page 32.*

# GLOSSARY

**confirmed**
Known for certain to be true or real.

**expeditions**
Long trips made to reach places or meet goals.

**Inuit**
People who are native to cold, northern parts of Canada, Alaska, and Greenland.

**investigations**
Work that is done to find out the truth about something.

**latitude**
A measure of how far north or south a place is.

**sextant**
A tool that allows people to use stars to find their way.

**snowmobiles**
Small vehicles that glide quickly over snow.

**Soviet**
Having to do with the Soviet Union, a country in Europe and Asia that existed from 1922 to 1991.

## BOOKS

Kirkman, Marissa. *Coldest Climates.* Mendota Heights, MN: Apex Editions, 2024.

Reynolds, A. M. *Matthew Henson*. North Mankato, MN: Capstone Publishing, 2021.

Rusick, Jessica. *Surviving the Arctic.* Minneapolis: Abdo Publishing, 2024.

## ONLINE RESOURCES

Visit **www.apexeditions.com** to find links and resources related to this title.

## ABOUT THE AUTHOR

Dalton Rains is an author and editor from Saint Paul, Minnesota.

# INDEX

**ANSWER KEY:**

1. Answers will vary; 2. Answers will vary; 3. B; 4. B; 5. C; 6. B